Harper Regan

Simon Stephens' play *Bluebird* was produced by the Royal Court in London in 1998. He was Pearson Writer-in-Residence at the Royal Exchange Theatre in 2000/1, and the Arts Council Resident Dramatist in 2000 at the Royal Court. His next play, *Herons* (Royal Court, 2001), was nominated for the Olivier Award for Most Promising Playwright. His radio play *Five Letters to Elizabeth* was broadcast on Radio 4 in 2001, and *Digging* on Radio 4 in 2003. His next stage play, *Port* (Royal Exchange, Manchester, 2002), was awarded the Pearson Award for Best New Play in 2001/2. *One Minute* was produced by the Actors' Touring Company, Sheffield, in June 2003; *Christmas* premiered at the Pavilion Theatre, Brighton, in the same year. Both plays transferred to the Bush Theatre, London, in 2004. *Country Music* was produced by the Royal Court in 2004. Subsequent plays include *On the Shore of the Wide World* (Royal Exchange and National Theatre, 2005; awarded Olivier Best Play 2005); *Motortown* (Royal Court, 2006; awarded the Theater Heute award for Best Foreign Playwright 2007); and *Pornography* (Deutsches Schauspielhaus, Hannover, 2007, invited to the Berlin Theater Treffen, 2008).

By the same author and available from Methuen Drama

Christmas
Country Music
Herons
Motortown
On the Shore of the Wide World
One Minute
Port

SIMON STEPHENS PLAYS: I
(Bluebird, Christmas, Herons, Port)

Simon Stephens

Harper Regan

Methuen Drama

Published by Methuen Drama 2008

1 3 5 7 9 10 8 6 4 2

Methuen Drama
A & C Black Publishers Limited
38 Soho Square
London W1D 3HB
www.acblack.com

Copyright © 2008 Simon Stephens

Simon Stephens has asserted his rights
under the Copyright, Designs and Patents Act, 1988,
to be identified as the author of this work

ISBN: 978 1 408 10151 3

A CIP catalogue record for this book is available
from the British Library.

Typeset by Country Setting, Kingsdown, Kent
Printed and bound in Great Britain
by Cox & Wyman Ltd, Reading Berkshire

For Mum and for Polly and for Scarlett

Harper Regan was first presented at the Cottesloe Theatre, National Theatre, London, on 23 April 2008. The cast, in order of appearance, was as follows:

Harper Regan	Lesley Sharp
Elwood Barnes	Michael Mears
Tobias Rich	Troy Glasgow
Seth Regan	Nick Sidi
Sarah Regan	Jessica Raine
Justine Ross	Jessica Harris
Mickey Nestor	Jack Deam
James Fortune	Brian Capron
Alison Woolley	Susan Brown
Duncan Woolley	Eamon Boland
Mahesh Aslam	Nitin Kundra

Director	Marianne Elliott
Designer	Hildegard Bechtler
Lighting Designer	Chris Davey
Sound Designer	Ian Dickinson

Harper Regan

Characters

Harper Regan
Elwood Barnes
Tobias Rich
Seth Regan
Sarah Regan
Justine Ross
Mickey Nestor
James Fortune
Alison Woolley
Duncan Woolley
Mahesh Aslam

Parts may be doubled as follows:
Elwood Barnes/Duncan Woolley
Tobias Rich/Mahesh Aslam
Seth Regan/James Fortune
Sarah Regan/Justine Ross

The play takes place in the late autumn of 2006 in Uxbridge and south Manchester.

Scene One

Harper Regan *and* **Elwood Barnes**.

Elwood's *office. The end of a Monday afternoon.*

Elwood If you go, I don't think you should come back.

A terribly long pause. As long as they can get away with. They stand incredibly still.

Harper I don't know what to say.

Elwood No.

Pause.

Harper I need to go home for a few days.

She waits for him to respond. He doesn't.

My dad's ill. He'd had something called a hypoglycaemic attack. He's gone into a coma. I need to go and see him. I've not seen him, I've not been back home for two years.

She waits for him to respond. He doesn't.

I never properly told him how much he meant to me.

Elwood That's not my concern.

Harper I've worked for thirty-four weeks without a single day off, not including bank holidays, and I don't think that's reasonable.

Elwood Harper, that's what you're paid to do. That's what everybody does.

That's in your contract.

Pause.

If it had been any other week.

He puts his hands in his pockets. Smiles at her. He moves a bit closer to her. She instinctively takes a step back away from him.

Harper, do you like it here?

Harper I don't know how to answer that.

Elwood Do you like this job?

Harper I . . .

Elwood It's not a trick question.

Harper I like you.

Elwood Thank you.

Harper I like working for you.

Elwood Well that's good.

Harper Some of the clients are quite friendly.

Elwood Aren't they?

Harper I think it's a nice office.

Elwood I think so too.

Harper There's a lovely view from your window.

Elwood *I* like that.

Harper You can see Heathrow. You can see Oxford on a good day.

Elwood Three contracts came through on Friday afternoon. You know that.

He moves away from her. He sits down.

Harper It would only be for a few days. A week at the most.

Elwood We have four days to complete the customs clearance on eight contracts outstanding from the summer. We have to clear the Bill of Lading applications on four others by next Monday.

He looks at her.

Harper That's not only my responsibility.

Elwood I can't just let you leave.

Pause.

He looks at her and then looks away.

How's Sarah?

Harper   She's fine, thank you.

Elwood   How old is she now?

Harper   She's seventeen.

Elwood   No!

Harper   She is. She's at college. She's doing her A levels. She's going to university next year hopefully.

Elwood   Poof! A little puff of smoke! Which A levels is she doing?

Harper   English, Geography and Religious Education.

Elwood   Proper subjects! With ideas in!

Harper   Yes.

Elwood   Big ideas. Huge ideas. There is a need for young people to embrace ideas. Young people today, Harper, they lack the energy to properly grapple with big ideas. Don't they?

She looks at him before she answers.

Harper   I don't know.

Elwood   They do. I know they do. I see them all the time. They wait outside Chimes, after it's closed. Their brains vacant from the lack of ideas. Making unusual noises to one another. Talking with their iPods still in. How do they do that?

Harper   I've no idea.

He turns back to her.

Elwood   I like Sarah. She wears remarkable clothes, I seem to remember.

Harper   I, yes.

Elwood   Will you give her my love?

Harper   I will.

Elwood   Does she need a job, do you think?

Harper   I don't know.

Elwood   If she does, will you tell her to call me, the second she realises?

Harper   Yes. I will.

Elwood   Do you know what frightens me about our young?

She looks at him again before she answers.

Harper   What, Mr Barnes?

Elwood   Their amorality.

He takes a big, long pause as he lets this settle in her head.

Not immorality, Harper. Not a wilful inability to act with a moral sense. An absolute absence of the thing in the first place. This is what is starting to infect our young. In England.

Pause.

It's your own fault, you know? Do you have the slightest idea how good you are at your job? You've become invaluable.

She pauses before she speaks.

Harper   Mr Barnes.

Elwood   Elwood. Call me Elwood, Harper, please.

Harper   Would you mind if I didn't?

Elwood   Why?

Harper   I'd call you by your first name if I thought you were my friend. You're my employer.

Pause.

If I don't go, I don't know what I'll do.

He smiles at her. She smiles back weakly.

I should be getting back.

Elwood   Don't.

Harper   What?

Elwood   You have a charming smile, Harper. When you answer the telephones, do you smile like that?

Harper   I don't know.

Elwood   I bet you do.

Harper   I –

Elwood   I imagine it has a remarkable impact. It must be why all these contracts keep pouring in. If you stopped smiling like that they'd all dry up, you know? You could have much more holiday. We all could. You could see your dad all the time. You could practically move in with the fucker.

Stay there. Stay exactly there. Stand exactly like that.

Harper   You're unnerving me a little, Mr Barnes I have to say.

Elwood   Yes. Now.

Silence. For thirty seconds.

Do you feel any better?

Harper   –

Elwood   Do you know what I just did?

Harper   –

Elwood   I counted out thirty seconds. In my head. One little second. Two little seconds. Three little seconds. And so on. That's what I do sometimes. I find a quiet place. To sit and count. It helps. Doesn't it?

Harper   I'm not sure.

Elwood   There aren't many quiet places left now, are there?

Harper   I quite like the canal.

Elwood   There's always a television. There's always a telephone. There's always a radio on. There's always music playing. There's always the internet, isn't there? Nowadays? Isn't there always the internet, Harper. There is. There's always the internet. The human being is a remarkable animal, Harper, don't you think?

Harper   I –

Elwood   It is an exceptional animal. It's the only animal, for example, which runs for pleasure! It's the only animal that does that! It is the only animal that has invented the internet. What was the last website you looked at, Harper?

He watches her think.

Harper   There's a website for The Slits that I like.

Elwood   The Slits?

Harper   They're a punk band. I like to find out what they're up to nowadays.

Elwood   Do you?

Harper   I met them once.

He looks at her. He is completely mystified.

Elwood   All of my shopping I do online. All of my reading I do online. All of my news I get online. All of my television I watch online. All of my radio I listen to online. I'm perpetually on YouTube watching videos of people having mishaps. I am obsessed with sports news. I read chat room after chat room about the English cricket team. I watch a measured amount of porn. Did you know that people can arrange illicit sexual encounters online nowadays? Honestly, Harper. You can go to these places. You can look at these things. This is actually happening. It's mostly men, of course, you have to say that. Men seek women. Man seeking woman.

Man seeking two women. No strings attached. I can't get enough of the things. I find them absolutely fascinating. Don't you?

Harper I don't know, Mr Barnes.

He watches her.

Elwood Do you know how many sick days I paid for last year? Sixty-seven.

Everybody's ill nowadays. Everybody's depressed. Everybody thinks they're ugly. Everybody's addicted to everything. Everybody has this tremendous amount of violence. I find it quite enthralling. It intoxicates me. I watch them all. They all scuttle off on holiday. 'Where are you going?' 'I'm going to the seaside!' 'Oh! I'm going to the seaside too!' 'What seaside are you going to?' '*This* seaside, what seaside are *you* going to?' '*That* seaside!'

Pause.

When the weather gets warm we move towards the water.

Pause.

He stands again.

I love this country. Don't you? Do you know how many freight vehicles I've got on the motorways of this country right now, at this second? I've got seventeen. They're all over the place. They're going everywhere. By the end of next week I'll have twenty-four.

She stares at him. She doesn't move or speak.

Do you know what I particularly love about this country, Harper?

She stares at him. She doesn't move or speak.

I love that it's all an accident of geography. The wealth of the place, the wealth of the pile, the mineral wealth of the lump is an accident of physical geography. The industrial revolution was an accident of physical geography. Our island isolationism is an accident of physical geography.

He smiles at her. Turns and looks out of his window.

Just when she thinks it's safe to move he starts again.

And have you ever asked yourself this? Why are there so few motorways east of the M1? Exactly what is happening to the East of England? It's eroding is what's happening. It's falling off. Poor souls.

He looks back out of the window.

Sometimes I have rather bleak thoughts.

He looks at her.

Elwood   How *is* Seth?

Harper   He's fine.

Elwood   And the job?

Harper   It's good. He likes it.

Elwood   A good practice?

Harper   He's happy there.

Elwood   Ecologically-friendly architecture. What exactly is that?

Harper   I don't really know.

Elwood   You know what these are, don't you?

Harper   What, what are?

Elwood   These are the final days of the Enlightenment is what these are. Don't laugh.

Harper   I wasn't laughing.

Elwood   I'm completely serious.

Harper   I know that.

Some time.

There is absolutely no way that you can have any time off.
Not now.

They look at each other.

What are you thinking about?

They look at each other.

Scene Two

The banks of the Grand Union Canal.

Tobias *and* **Harper**.

Harper James?

Tobias What?

Harper Oh God.

Tobias *stares at her.*

Harper I'm sorry. You're not James, are you?

Tobias Who?

Harper I thought you were somebody else. You look like
somebody I know. You look a bit like my nephew. I'm sorry.
I'm embarrassed now.

He stares at her for a bit, then looks away.

I'm always doing that. Do you ever do that?

Tobias No.

Harper Don't you? I do it all the time.

He looks at her. He says nothing. He looks away.

Do you ever get that sense that you're just one big awful
embarrassing lump?

Tobias   No.

A long pause.

Harper   It's getting dark.

Tobias   Who *are* you?

Harper   I'm sorry. I'm Harper. Harper Regan.

He looks at her, says nothing.

I live on Church Lane. I come here every night. Every night on my way home I come here and stand on this bridge and have a bit of a look.

He looks at her, says nothing.

I've not seen you before. I wasn't looking where I was going. My mind was completely elsewhere. And I saw you and you looked like my nephew, James. My husband's nephew, really. And then I got closer and you're nothing at all like him. Which is embarrassing for me and probably for you but there you are.

He looks away from her, says nothing.

A long silence. Neither move.

It goes all the way to Birmingham.

Tobias   What does?

Harper   The canal.

He looks at her. He looks away. He looks at her again. He looks away again.

A pause.

Tobias   Have you ever been there?

Harper   What? Where? Birmingham? No. No I haven't. No.

A pause.

Tobias   I always wanted to go. And then somebody I know went and he said it was shit.

He grins.

Harper   Yes. I heard that.

She smiles.

Tobias   I like it at this time of day. It looks like a mirror. I've seen it in lots of different places around London. I like it here the best.

A pause. She examines him.

Harper   How old are you?

Tobias   What?

Harper   I just wanted to know how old you are.

Tobias   Why?

Harper   I was thinking about something.

Tobias   I'm seventeen.

Harper   You don't look seventeen.

Tobias   I am.

Harper   Are you from round here?

Tobias   Yeah. What were you thinking about?

Harper   From Uxbridge?

Tobias   Yeah. Why?

Harper   Are you at the college, are you, or something like that?

Tobias   Yes, I am.

Harper   My daughter goes there.

Tobias   For real?

Harper   Sarah. She's called. Sarah Regan. Do you know her?

Tobias   No.

Harper   Are you sure? She's from Manchester.

Tobias   Like Manchester United?

Harper   What?

Tobias   They're from Manchester.

A beat.

Harper   We only came down two years ago. She's very pretty. She wears a lot of black. She's a bit of a Goth.

Tobias   I don't know any Goths.

Harper   She might know you. I'll ask her. What's your name?

Tobias   Tobias.

Harper   Is it? Tobias what?

Tobias   Rich.

Harper   Tobias Rich? (*Beat.*) I'll ask her if she knows you.

Tobias (*smiling*)   I doubt it.

Harper   Why?

Tobias   People don't know me.

Harper   What do you mean?

Tobias   They don't. Goths definitely don't know me. People don't like me. None of them.

Harper   Why's that?

Tobias   Just. Reasons.

Harper   I see. (*Beat.*) Where do you live?

Tobias   Waterloo Road.

Harper   That's close.

Tobias   It's my dad's house.

A slight pause.

He's never in. Ever.

A pause. She looks at him.

Harper   Where's your Mum?

Tobias   In Cardiff.

Harper   Cardiff's meant to be a good place.

Tobias   Right.

Pause.

Harper   Do you miss her?

Tobias   Who?

Harper   Your mum.

Tobias   Fuck off.

Pause.

She looks at him to check if he's lying.

Harper   You shouldn't swear at people.

He moves away from her a little.

What is it that you're doing? At college?

Tobias   Engineering.

Harper   Do you enjoy it?

He looks at her for a while before he answers.

Tobias   I do, yeah. (*Beat.*) I find it a bit confusing.

Harper   I know that feeling!

Tobias   Just the way they work.

Harper   Engines?

Tobias   It's a bit . . . I don't know. It exhausts me.

Harper   What does?

Tobias   The course. The engines. The college. The people there.

Harper   I see.

Tobias   I mean, I'm good, you know? I work hard. I do my lessons. I'm quiet. I don't say much. But sometimes.

Pause.

They smile at each other.

Why are you talking to me?

Harper   I just. I'm sorry. Do you want me to go?

Tobias   No. It's not that. It's just. Girls don't normally talk to me.

Harper   Why not?

Tobias   I never know what to say to them. I stand there gawping. They ask me what I'm gawping at. I can't say 'You'. Can I? Can I though?

Harper   No.

Tobias   They think I smell. Do you think I smell?

Harper   No.

Tobias   I do, you know?

Harper   Do you?

Tobias   Everybody does.

Harper   Yes.

Tobias   Everybody has their own smell. It's a kind of homing device. But I hate mine. It's completely rank. I hate my smell. I hate my hair. I hate my bedroom. You wanna see my bedroom?

Harper   Not really, probably. No.

Tobias   It's the dumbest bedroom. It's lame. It's a ridiculous bedroom. The only thing I like about me is my bike.

Harper   What kind of bike have you got?

Tobias   It's a Ridgeback Nemesis. It's a hybrid. It's got hub gears. It's perfect for the city. It's completely proper. I'm fucking fast on it.

Harper   There you go again.

He looks at her before he continues.

Tobias   I'm the fastest boy in London. I go past all the other people, on their bikes. I'm faster than all of them. In my head it's like I'm racing.

Harper   Do you wear a helmet?

Tobias   Yeah.

Harper   That's good. That's important. Do you wear it over your cap?

Beat.

He examines her.

Tobias   You're not Polish, are you?

Harper   I'm not what?

Tobias   I hate the Poles. All of them, round here. They fucking deserve it.

He breaks into a grin.

My dad properly looks after me. If he knew I was here! He'd ask me very difficult questions about you; I can tell you that for nothing. He'd say you shouldn't be here. He doesn't think it's right.

Harper   'Right'?

Tobias   He thinks women should be at home. Should look after their children. You see the way the women dress in this country. I think it's better to be covered up. You see little kids. Little ten-year-old kids and they're dressed like that.

Harper   Like what?

Tobias   You can't move in the street for women all dressed up with their clothes and their skirts and their make-up and I think you should be ashamed of yourselves. Nobody believes in God round here, is one thing. If you don't believe in God, then how are you meant to know what to do? How are you meant to know how to live? You don't. I think that must be terrible.

A silence.

She looks at him. She looks away when she thinks he might see her looking at him.

She takes out a bottle of mineral water and opens it and drinks from it.

Harper   I wanted to talk to somebody.

Beat.

I don't really know anybody around here.

Beat.

I've had a bit of a strange day.

Beat.

My dad's ill. I wanted some time off work. To go and see him. I couldn't get it. My boss was a bit odd.

He looks back at her.

Tobias   You should go anyway.

People should see their fathers. They should respect them.

You'll regret it if you don't.

Harper   Yeah.

A long pause.

Tobias   I like you.

Harper   I'm sorry?

Tobias   In case you were worried about that.

Harper   Thank you.

Tobias   I like older women as a rule. I like white women and I like older women. The idea of an older white woman is almost like a kind of dream, to me.

She says nothing.

You seem a bit sad though, you know?

Harper   Sad?

Tobias   You do a little.

Harper   I don't know about sad. (*Beat.*) Do you want some of my water?

Tobias   What?

Harper   Here.

Tobias   Thanks.

She passes him a bottle of water.

She watches him drink it.

Harper   That's nice.

Tobias   What?

Harper   I like the way you drink. I like the way you raise your drink up to your mouth. There's something in the way you hold the bottle to your lips.

Scene Three

Harper's *kitchen.*

Seth *and* **Sarah.**

Seth   OK.

He looks at her, thinks.

What are glaciers?

Sarah   Glaciers are huge sheets of moving ice.

He smiles at her.

Thinks.

Seth   What effect does their movement have?

Sarah   They erode the land.

Seth   Good. How much of the earth's fresh water do they hold?

Sarah   Seventy-five per cent.

Seth   Very good. How long can they grow up to?

Sarah   One hundred kilometres. These are easy, do a hard one.

Seth   How do they form?

Sarah   Glaciers begin to form when snow accumulates and remains in an area all year round. If temperatures don't rise enough to completely melt the snow, snow continues to accumulate. Each year, new layers of snow bury and compress the previous layers. The weight of the overlying snow puts enough pressure on the bottommost snow-layers to compress them into large, thickened ice masses. This compression forces the snow to re-crystallise. During re-crystallisation, the crystals interlock to create ice that essentially behaves like rock. Once a mass of compressed ice reaches a critical thickness, it becomes so heavy that it begins to move.

A long pause.

He stares at her.

Seth   You sound like a textbook.

Sarah   What?

Seth   You sound like you've memorised something.

Sarah   I have.

Seth   Not like you know it.

Sarah   I do.

Seth   It doesn't sound like that.

Sarah   It doesn't need to.

Seth   Not for your exam, maybe, but for, like, your life!

Sarah   I'm not bothered about that.

Seth   What?

Sarah   I'm not.

Seth   You're not bothered about life!

Sarah   Dad.

Seth   That's what you just said.

Sarah   I didn't mean –

Seth   How can you not be bothered about life?

Sarah   I am. It's just my exams are more immediately pressing. Ask me something else. Go on. Ask me anything.

Seth   Listen to you.

Sarah   What do you want to know about? Internal deformation? Easy. Basal sliding? Piece of piss.

Seth   Sarah!

Sarah   What is deforming substrate? I could deform substrate with my eyes closed!

Seth   I'm sure you could.

Sarah   Ice sheets. Ice caps. Ice fields. Ice shelves. Mountain glaciers. Tidewater glaciers. Hanging glaciers. Terminal moraines. Lateral moraines. Ground moraines. Medial moraines. Drumlins. Eskers. Kettle holes. Kettle ponds. Kettle lakes. Ask me anything.

Seth   How was college?

Sarah   What?

Seth   Today?

Sarah   It was fine.

Seth   Do you like it there?

Beat.

Do you? Does it make you happy?

Sarah   Dad, you're being weird.

Seth   I'm sorry.

Sarah   'Does it make you happy?' You sound like a counsellor.

Seth   I worry about you settling in down here. I worry about you working too hard.

Sarah   You don't need to.

Seth   That won't necessarily stop me.

Sarah   Well, it should.

Seth   After everything I put you and your mum through.

Sarah   Dad, don't.

Beat.

College was fine. It *is* fine. I like it. It's full of people. It's so completely full of people that sometimes it's actually rather difficult to move in there. The overwhelming majority of them are complete strangers to me. I'm very glad about this because

I have to say that I find most of them odious and most of the
rest ridiculous. There are about three people who I like. But
I like them enormously. The teachers nearly all look like they're
on the cusp of some kind of a nervous breakdown. I think they
thought sixth form would be easy. They didn't bank on sixth
formers being like third years but much, much bigger and with
better weapons and more chaotic hormones. There are about
two teachers who are fucking magic but that's not that bad a
ratio all things considered.

Seth   Not at all.

Sarah   The coffee machines are terrible.

Seth   Bastard.

Sarah   I know. But they sell really good chicken nuggets in
the canteen and I've discovered that if you stuff them with
skittles you get a really fantastic buzz.

Seth   I'll have to try that.

Sarah   Do. It keeps me going all day.

Harper *enters.*

Harper   Hi.

Sarah   Hi, Mum.

Seth   Hello, sweetheart.

Harper   How are you, lovely?

Sarah   I'm fine. I'm good. My knowledge of the formation
and movement of glaciers is so absolutely overwhelming it
amazes even me.

Harper   Very good.

Sarah   Can I ask you something?

Harper   Go on.

Sarah   Don't you think Dad looks stupid?

Harper What?

Sarah In his suit?

Harper I don't know.

Sarah He does. You do. You look really, really nice in jeans. And you look absolutely oafish in your suit.

Harper Oafish?

Seth She's been saying this to me all day.

Harper I can imagine.

Sarah Wear. Jeans. All. The. Time.

Seth I'm forty-three.

Sarah So?

Seth I can't wear jeans all the time. I'd look pathetic. Have you eaten?

Harper No.

Seth I was going to cook, are you hungry?

Sarah I'm going out.

Seth I wasn't asking you. Why would I ask you?

Sarah Lovely. See. Isn't he?

Harper What were you cooking?

Seth Sesame beef and asparagus stir-fry.

Sarah Wow.

Seth See! 'I'm going out'!

Sarah How do you do that?

Seth You get your beef. You sesame it. You get your asparagus. You put them together. In a big wok. Fry 'em up. Bob's your uncle.

Harper That sounds lovely.

Sarah   You look really tired, Mum.

Harper   Thank you.

Sarah   You do, you look awful.

Harper   I've had quite a day.

Sarah   Why?

Harper   Just. Mr Barnes says hello.

Sarah   Right. 'Hello, Mr Barnes.'

Harper   He told me to tell you that if you want a job you should just ask him.

Sarah   Did he?

Harper   He seemed quite taken by the idea. Where are you going?

Sarah   What?

Harper   Tonight?

Sarah   I'm going to Lola's. And then we're going out to the White Horse. It's her birthday. We might go to Sub2000.

Seth   Fabulous.

Sarah   You want to come?

Harper   It's a school night.

Sarah   You don't go to school any more.

Harper   Seriously, Sarah.

Sarah   What?

Harper   You've got your exams.

Sarah   Mum!

Harper   They're months away.

Sarah   Do you think I don't know that?

Harper   No. of course I don't. I didn't mean that.

Sarah   Do you think I don't think about them, all the time? Honestly.

Harper   No, I know.

Sarah   You should cut my head open. If you cut my head open right now and had a good old look at it you'd see, running right through it, like a stick of rock. EXAMS.

Seth   That sounds really painful.

Harper   Seth.

Seth   Sorry.

Harper   I just don't want you to come home at two o'clock in the morning and have to get up at eight and have to turn your brain on because I think you'd get tired. And if you do it too often you'd wear yourself out. And I don't want you to wear yourself out and then not do as well as you could do in your exams because you'd regret it.

Sarah   I don't.

Harper   What?

Sarah   I don't do that. I hardly ever go out in the week.

Harper   I –

Sarah   I hardly ever go out at all. Full stop. The end.

Harper   Yeah.

Sarah *leaves.*

Harper   Shit.

A pause.

Seth   She's all right.

Harper   I know. I'll go up.

Seth   She won't, you know?

Harper   What?

Seth   Do what you said.

Harper   No.

Sarah *comes back. She is wearing a leather jacket.*

Sarah   Ask him how good I was. If you don't believe me.

She leaves again. This time, through the front door.

They let her departure settle.

Seth   She was.

Harper   I'm sure.

Seth   She was pretty amazing. She sounded a bit odd. But she knows it all.

Harper   Yeah. I'll go after her.

Seth   Do you know where she's going?

Harper   I think so.

Seth   Did he say no?

Harper   Yeah.

Seth   Right.

Harper   I don't know what to do. Bastard.

Seth   Harper.

Harper   Honestly, Seth, you should have seen him. The way he looked at me. He just goes on and on and on. He's weird. He's horrible. He makes me want to tell him to stuff his job up his arse. And walk out and go anyway.

Seth   You can't.

Harper   I know. I'm not an idiot.

Pause.

Seth   Do you want a hug?

Harper   No. I'm all right.

Seth   Are you sure?

Harper   Yes.

Seth   What time do you want to eat?

Harper   I could get another job.

He looks at her.

I go past windows. There are adverts for jobs all over the place. Look in the newspaper. I could get a better job. I could get more money. I don't think it matters about my qualifications.

Seth   Don't you?

Harper   Not with my experience.

He says nothing.

Look. I know. All right. Don't look at me like that.

He says nothing.

How was your day?

Seth   You know.

Harper   What did you do?

Seth   I went to Thompson's. Got the light bulbs for the hallway.

Went to Wong's. Got the sesame seeds.

Some little tyke tried to push me off my bicycle. Seriously. Don't laugh. He was a vicious little prick. He walked as though he was from Harlem. I told him you're not. You're from Uxbridge. There's a difference.

I came back home. Inspector Ritter popped round. He says hello.

I tidied the study a bit. I went online. Did my emails.

Harper   Did you?

Seth   Don't, Harper.

Harper   Don't what?

Seth   Just. I did some research into glacial movement.
Tested Sarah.

Harper   She's right about your suit, you know?

Seth   I know.

Harper   You should just wear your jeans. You do look nice
in them.

He looks at her.

Seth   Do you want some wine?

Harper   I'm all right.

Seth   Are you sure?

Harper   Yeah. I should go and find Sarah.

They look at each other for a time.

Seth   Would you mind if I put the radio on?

Harper   No. No. No. I'm in your way.

Seth   You're not.

Harper   I am.

Seth   It's not that.

Harper   I'll move. I'll go now. I won't be long.

*She stands still for a short time. They have no idea what to say to each
other.*

Scene Four

A recreational ground behind Church Lane. **Sarah** *and* **Harper**.

Sarah *is eating a stick of celery.*

Harper *shows her a piece of masonry.*

Harper   This just fell on me.

Sarah   What?

Harper   When I came out. When I was looking for you. It's masonry. It nearly hit me. It could have killed me.

Sarah   Where did it come from?

Harper   From . . . up there, somewhere. I have no idea.

Sarah *examines it. She gives it back.*

Harper   It was frightening.

Sarah *says nothing.*

Harper   Be careful, won't you? Coming here.

Sarah *says nothing.*

Harper   Those buildings aren't safe. Clearly.

Sarah *says nothing.*

Harper   What are you eating?

Sarah   Celery.

Harper   Celery?

Sarah   Celery's good for you. I like it. It tastes nice.

Harper *smiles and looks at her.* **Sarah** *offers her a stick of celery.* **Harper** *takes it. She eats it.*

Harper   I'm sorry. For earlier. It was stupid of me.

Sarah   Yeah. It was.

Harper   I was worried and I shouldn't have been.

Sarah   I just want you to trust me a bit.

Harper   I do trust you, Sarah. Of course I do.

Sarah   You've got a funny way of showing it.

Harper   I'm just tired.

Sarah   Yeah.

Harper   I've had an awful day. I won't do it again.

Sarah *looks at her, weighing up whether to believe her or not.*

Harper   You go out tonight. Please. Here.

She reaches into her pocket. She finds a purse. She takes forty pounds from it. She gives it to **Sarah***.*

Harper   Have this. Spend it. Have fun. OK?

Sarah *takes it.*

Sarah   Thank you.

Harper   I'm such an idiot.

Sarah   It's OK.

Harper   I'm sorry.

Sarah   I accept your apology.

Harper *smiles.* **Sarah** *smiles back.*

Sarah   Thank you for apologising.

Harper *smiles. She becomes rather pleased.*

Harper   Thank you for accepting it.

They sit.

They watch a flock of birds fly overhead.

Sarah   What did Mr Barnes say about you going away?

Harper   He told me I couldn't go.

Sarah   Shit.

Harper   Yeah.

Sarah   Wanker.

Harper *looks at her, slightly crossly, for a beat.*

Harper   Yeah. How was college?

Sarah   It was fine.

Harper   What did you do?

Sarah *looks as though she is about to laugh.*

Harper   What? What's funny?

Sarah   Nothing.

Pause.

Harper   I think it's good that you do geography.

Sarah   Good?

Harper   I wish I'd done geography. I wish I knew about the world a bit more. I wish I'd been to more places.

Pause.

Do you know what the furthest place I've ever been to is?

Beat.

Italy. When I was little we used to go camping in Tuscany. Most kids went on holiday to England in those days. I've never been any further since.

Pause.

I don't even speak Italian.

Pause.

I've never been on a long-haul flight. Which is probably a good thing. I hate flying. I get scared.

Sarah   Mum.

Harper   Sarah.

Sarah   What are you going on about?

Harper   I'm sorry. I'll go back.

Pause. She looks at the masonry for a bit.

Do you think it would have killed me?

Sarah   Depends on the distance it fell from. The trajectory.

Harper   Yes. It's a bit unsettling. You think you know where you are and then . . .

Pause.

I like your jacket.

Sarah   Thanks.

Harper   Where did you get that?

Sarah   In town.

Harper   I've not seen it before.

Sarah   I only got it last week.

Harper   I always wanted a leather jacket.

Sarah   Did you?

Harper   I never had one. I wouldn't get one now. I'd look stupid. It's funny.

Sarah   What?

Harper   I'm forty-one.

Sarah   Yeah?

Harper   It kind of creeps up on you. Just when you least expect it, you get old.

Sarah   You're not old.

Harper   What were you listening to?

Sarah   Arcade Fire.

Harper   See?

Sarah   What?

Harper   Who in God's name are Arcade Fire?

Sarah *smiles.*

Harper   Don't laugh. I used to have a Rickenbacker, you know?

Sarah   A what?

Harper   It's a guitar. The same one Johnny Marr had.

Sarah   Who?

Harper   Never mind. I am so weird, aren't I? Am I a huge embarrassment to you?

Sarah *thinks.*

Sarah   Not a huge one.

Harper   A little one. A quite big one.

Sarah   You're just a bit odd.

Harper   I met somebody from your college today. Tobias Rich. Do you know him?

Sarah *shakes her head.*

Harper   Do you like the people you go to college with?

Sarah   They're all right.

Harper   Are they different to your old mates?

Sarah *looks at her before she answers.*

Sarah   They're a bit more stupid.

Harper *smiles.*

Sarah   They talk absolute bollocks an awful lot of the time. But that's only to be expected.

Harper   Right.

Sarah   Do you know what they were talking about today?

Harper   I've no idea.

Sarah   They were talking about how cool life will be in a hundred years time.

Harper   Great.

Sarah   Do you know what I think life will be like in a hundred years time?

Harper   What?

Sarah   I think it'll be completely fucked.

Harper *gives her a look.*

Sarah   You did ask.

Harper   Yeah. (*Beat.*) I hope not.

Harper *looks at her masonry.*

She throws it away.

Sarah *lights a cigarette.*

Sarah   In three days the planet's going to go into the ecological red. We'll have used up all the energy resources that the planet can provide for this current population this year. For the next three months everything else is building up a debt. Each year this point of saturation gets earlier. Fuck knows when it will be if the population makes it to ten billion. Which it will.

Pause.

Harper *looks a bit bewildered.*

Sarah   As a species we are killing ourselves. Do you know how long it's taken us?

Harper *looks at her for an answer.*

Sarah   A hundred thousand years at the absolute longest. That's nothing, Mum.

Harper   Isn't it?

Sarah   Most of the destruction happened over the last six thousand. The majority in the last fifty. On a planet four and a half billion years old.

She puts her cigarette out. She immediately lights another one.

Do you know what makes me really cross?

Harper   What?

Sarah   We did this today. 'The Theory of Grand Design.'

Harper   The what?

Sarah   The idea that the fact that we are here, that human beings are on this planet, is down to such a remarkable series of interconnected phenomena that it could only have been brought about by God. He designed it. He did a grand job. Do you know why it makes me cross?

Harper   I have absolutely no idea.

Sarah   Because it's based on the idea that humans are perfect. We're not. We're a complete unholy mess.

She finishes her cigarette.

Harper *looks at her.*

They sit for a bit.

Sarah   I'm going to live in the country. Be a farmer. Grow really long hair. Right down my back. Get some wellies. Walk about in them.

Harper   Get a Labrador.

Sarah   Good thinking.

Harper   Can I come?

Sarah   You can visit.

Harper   Thanks.

Pause.

Do you know what I like about you?

Sarah   What's that?

Harper   You're very confident.

Pause.

You know your dad?

Sarah   Yeah, what about him?

Harper   I love him very much.

I wanted to tell you. I like our family. I think it's a good one. Don't you?

Sarah *thinks.*

Sarah   I sometimes wish I had a brother.

Harper   Do you?

Sarah   I've said it now.

Harper   I just wanted you.

Sarah   Yeah.

Silence.

I'm sorry he's ill. Grandad.

Harper   Thank you.

Sarah   Diabetes is fucking horrible.

Harper   Yeah, it is.

Sarah   I'm still really cross with them.

Harper   Yes. It was Mum more than him. He would never have said anything without her forcing him to.

Sarah   Maybe.

Pause.

Are you going to go anyway? To see him?

Harper *doesn't look at her.*

Sarah   That means you are, doesn't it?

Harper *doesn't look at her.*

Scene Five

A small room in Stepping Hill Hospital, Stockport. Tuesday morning.

Harper Regan *and* **Justine Ross**.

Justine   Where have you come up from?

Harper   London. Just outside.

Justine   I've never been – to London, I mean.

Harper   You should go.

Justine   I never fancied it.

A slight pause.

Are you staying with your mum?

Harper   No. I'm . . . in a hotel.

Justine   Right.

Harper   We don't, me and my mum, we haven't always got on.

Justine   Is there nobody else you can stay with?

Harper   I don't really know anybody up here any more.

A slight pause.

Nobody knows I'm here.

A slight pause.

I hate hospitals.

Justine Do you?

Harper I'm stupid. I'm scared of getting cancer.

Justine Well, that's not all that stupid.

Harper It is, when you think about it. Hospitals are where they cure you of cancer, not where you contract it.

Justine Yes.

Pause.

I should tell you. I spoke to your mum, this morning. She's still down as his next of kin. He'd asked not to change that. So a lot of the procedures she'll be responsible for unless she waives that responsibility or you volunteer to take it on and persuade her to let you do that.

Harper Right.

Justine She said she'd come in with Duncan, probably tomorrow. Is Duncan her . . . ?

Harper He's her second husband, yes.

Justine He seems nice. On the phone.

Harper Yes.

Pause.

Justine It's an unusual name isn't it? Harper?

Harper I don't know. It was my dad's idea.

Justine 'There ain't one thing in this world I can do about folks except laugh, so I'm gonna join the circus and laugh my head off.'

Harper *smiles at her.*

Harper Do you do this a lot?

Justine Sometimes.

Harper Do you need to go back to work now?

Justine   No.

Harper   I thought you'd be rushed off your feet.

Justine   I can wait here as long as you want me to.

Harper   Do they pay you to do that? Is it part of the job description?

Justine   It is, actually.

Harper   How old are you?

Justine   Twenty-seven.

Harper   You look very young for twenty-seven.

Justine *smiles.*

Pause.

Harper   Is it too late to even see him?

Justine *doesn't answer.*

Harper   Do you know what I wanted to do?

Justine   What's that?

Harper   I wanted to see his leg. I wanted to put my finger in his wound. Underneath it.

Pause.

What happened?

A slight pause.

Talk me through what happened.

Justine   His condition deteriorated very rapidly. He was already in a full coma by the time he got here. The levels of critical insulin in his blood were so low. He didn't wake up. He didn't suffer any pain. He was asleep when he died.

Harper   Would he have felt it at all?

Justine   I don't think so.

Harper   But you don't know.

Justine   As far as we can tell he wouldn't.

Harper   But it's not a guarantee.

Justine   It can't be.

Harper   So he might have done.

Justine   I don't know that.

Harper   Oh dear.

She sobs once.

Justine   I'm sorry.

Harper *smiles at her.*

Harper   What do you think it would have been like?

Justine   I don't think he would have been conscious.

Harper   So it would have been like he was dreaming?

Justine   Maybe.

Harper   And then the dream just stops. Do you think he would have felt himself stopping breathing?

Justine   It's hard to say.

Harper   Like he dreamt he was drowning and then in real life he was.

Justine   We can't tell.

Harper   Can't you tell anything? Aren't there tests?

Justine   Probably he would have sensed the lights in the room. He might have recognised sounds.

Harper   Was he on his own?

Justine *looks at her.*

Harper   Was he on his own?

Justine *looks at her.*

Harper   Was he on his own when he died?

Justine   Yes, he was. I'm sorry.

Harper *bursts out crying.*

Justine *offers her a tissue.*

Justine   Here.

Harper   Get off. I don't want a tissue. A fucking tissue!

Justine *puts the tissue down between them.*

Justine   I'm sorry.

Harper *cries.*

She talks to try and gather herself.

Harper   I flew up last night. I'll lose my job now. My husband can't work. We have to borrow money so that my daughter can go to university and the interest on the repayment is just crippling and I asked my boss if I could come and he said no and I came anyway so now we've just, we've had it, basically. My husband has no idea where I am.

Some time. She dries her eyes with her hand. And then with the tissue.

I never told him how much I loved him.

Justine   No.

Harper   How horrible is that?

Justine   It's not.

Harper   It is, you know.

Justine   It's surprisingly normal.

Harper   What?

Justine   In my experience. He wouldn't have wanted you to worry about that.

Harper   Don't patronise me.

Justine   I'm not patronising you. You'd love your daughter even if she never told you how much she loved you. Wouldn't you? My mum and dad love me so much sometimes it gets a bit oppressive and I've never told them anything of the sort.

Harper   I can't believe this is happening.

Pause.

I should get going, shouldn't I?

Justine   You don't need to.

Harper   No, but you want me to. I can tell that just by looking at your eyes.

Justine   I don't.

Some time.

What are you going to do today?

Harper   Do?

Justine   For the rest of your day? Have you thought? Have you got plans?

Harper   I'm going to go and steal a car. Go joy-riding. I've never been joy-riding. I bet it's a lot easier than you imagine, isn't it?

Justine   Yes. No. I don't know.

Harper   I'm not really.

Justine   No.

Harper   I'll probably go for a drink.

Justine   Right. It's ten o'clock in the morning.

Harper   Yes.

Justine   Be careful, won't you?

Harper   Yes. Of course.

Justine   If you want, there's a chapel in the hospital. With a chaplain. It is multi-denominational. If that would help. A lot of people find that it does. More people go there than you'd think. I go sometimes. On my lunch break. I find it quite comforting. I go quite a lot, actually. But I'm a bit. I go to church every Sunday too. I go to see United every Saturday and to church every Sunday. My parents think I'm crackers. They don't go. I'm the only Christian in my family. Which is unusual, I think.

Harper *looks at her.*

Justine   Just 'cause I go to church doesn't mean I disapprove of people having a drink every now and then, by the way.

Harper   No. I didn't think that it did.

Justine   I go out and get drunk sometimes.

Harper   Do you?

Justine   I'm a bit of an embarrassment when I'm drunk. I get quite giggly. Fall over. Start singing. 'We are Ferguson's army! The cocks of the North!'

They smile together.

I just don't want –

Pause.

Is there anything else you want to ask me?

Harper   I can't think.

Justine   No. I know that feeling.

Harper   Have you ever had sex with a complete stranger?

Justine   What? I didn't mean. I meant.

Harper   Yeah. I'm sorry.

A very long pause.

Justine   I hate my job sometimes.

Harper   I'm, that's a shame.

Justine   They keep telling me that I have to keep a distance. I'm rubbish at it. I wish I could just leave it. Get another job. Get a better flat. My flat's really messy.

A long pause.

This weather's quite strange isn't it?

Harper   It is a bit.

Justine   It's so warm. For this time of year. After the summer we had. It'll break soon, probably. There'll be a storm.

Scene Six

A pub. It is raining heavily outside.

Harper *drinks a glass of white wine.*

Mickey Nestor *drinks a large glass of whisky.*

They sit for a while.

He looks at her. Looks away. Drinks. Smiles. Looks at her again for a long time.

She doesn't notice anything.

Mickey   I like your shoulders.

She is startled out of her reverie.

Harper   What?

Mickey   You've got very attractive shoulders. That's quite an unusual quality in a woman.

She looks at him for a while before answering. As though he's spoken in a different language.

Harper   Thank you.

Mickey   That's all right.

Beat.

Are you here on your own?

No response.

That means you are.

He grins.

Can I get you another drink?

Harper   No thank you.

Mickey   It's eleven o'clock in the morning. Did you know that?

No response.

Not many people come here on their own at eleven o'clock in the morning and have the dignity to turn down a free drink when one's offered.

No response.

I'm Mickey.

She looks up at him.

Long pause.

Harper   Hello, Mickey.

Mickey   Hello.

She looks away again.

He watches her.

What's your name?

Harper   Harper.

Mickey   Is it really?

Harper   Yeah.

Mickey   Do you want a cigarette, Harper?

Harper   No, thank you.

Mickey   Do you not smoke?

Harper   No, I don't.

Mickey   Good for you.

He takes out a cigarette and goes to light it. She looks around her for bar staff to stop him. He notices. Grins. Puts his fingers to his lips and whispers to her to:

Mickey   Ssshhh. Don't tell anybody.

Harper   I've always hated smoking.

Mickey   Is that right?

Harper   In men especially. I think it can be quite elegant in women sometimes. I think it makes men stink.

He looks at her. Smiles. She looks away.

Mickey   What kind of a name is Harper?

No response.

I'm trying to start a conversation here! Is that a crime? Fucking hell!

She looks up. Looks back down again.

Where do you live, Harper?

Harper   In London.

Mickey   It speaks! Whereabouts in London do you live?

Harper   Uxbridge.

Mickey   Uxbridge isn't in London. Uxbridge is fucking miles out of London, Harper. Fucking hell.

She looks at him. Looks away again.

He never stops looking at her.

Pause.

Mickey   What brings you up here?

Harper   I came up for a holiday.

Mickey   To Stockport?

Harper   Yeah.

Mickey   Good thinking.

Harper   My parents live up here.

Mickey   Right.

Pause.

He smiles.

I hate my parents.

Harper   Do you?

Mickey   They fucking do my head in. Gibbering on.

Harper   Yeah.

Mickey   And my friends. I hate my friends and all. The only good thing about my friends is watching them get drunk. Sometimes, on a good night, they roll about all over the place. That's always quite entertaining.

Harper   It sounds it.

Mickey   I'm going to get some new ones.

Harper   How are you going to do that?

Mickey   I haven't got a clue.

He drinks. Lights another cigarette. Smokes for a while.

I'm thirty next year. Is it incredibly depressing?

Harper   What?

Mickey   Being thirty.

Harper   How do you know I have the slightest idea?

Mickey   Oh, come on!

He laughs a little. Leans into her.

She looks away.

Pause.

Harper   I did get a bit depressed, actually.

Mickey   I can imagine.

Harper   I wasn't expecting to. And then I woke up in the morning. It took me by surprise a bit.

He grins.

Mickey   I bet I can guess your job.

Harper   I bet you can't.

Mickey   I bet you're a teacher.

Harper   No.

Mickey   A solicitor.

She says nothing.

A politician.

Harper   No.

Mickey   Do you know what I do?

Harper   No.

Mickey   I'm a journalist.

She says nothing.

I write for the *Messenger.*

Harper   What's that like?

Mickey   It's completely fucking shite.

Harper   Is it?

Mickey   I spent yesterday in court. This woman got fined
£150 for stealing seven ladders. She stole them from a yard
down her street. She took them back herself. Nobody has any
idea why. I covered her trial. After that I went to interview this
other couple that had a firework put through their letterbox.
That was quite funny as it goes. She kept stammering. This
woman from Levenshulme's just released a book about
microwave dieting. I spent most of the rest of the day at her
fucking book launch. Eating microwaved food samples and
drinking her wine.

Harper *looks away.*

Mickey   They're getting rid of journalists.

Harper   Are they?

Mickey   They're getting rid of people in the news industry,
on the whole. I don't blame them. They can Google all the
news they need. Cut and paste it. Get shot of the middle man.

No response.

*He reaches into his inside pocket. He takes out a small snuffbox. He
snorts some cocaine from it.*

You want some?

Harper   What is it?

Mickey   Fucking sherbet dib-dab what does it look like?

Harper   No, thank you.

Mickey   Suit yourself.

Harper   Don't they mind?

Mickey   What?

Harper   You, doing that in here?

Mickey   Does it look like they mind?

He lets it settle. He smiles.

He looks at her.

Some time.

She smiles.

Harper   Can I call you Michael, instead of Mickey?

Mickey   Why?

Harper   Mickey sounds like a little boy's name.

He sniffs a big sniff and wipes his nose on his sleeve.

Mickey   Do you know what fascinates me?

Harper   What's that?

Mickey   Surveillance.

Harper   You what?

Mickey   Do you know how many people are watching your computer at any one given time?

Harper   What are you talking about?

Mickey   Do you know how they do it?

Harper   I don't have a computer.

Mickey   They read the words that you type into your keyboard. I don't mind. It doesn't bother me. The fraud's a bit of a drag but frankly, can you blame people? Wouldn't you? You know what I mean.

Pause.

I mean, I think people should just be a bit more honest about it. They should go on radio phone-ins and just fucking say, 'I like porn! I look at it all the time! There's nothing I like more than watching images of twenty-year-old mid-western girls fucking older men. Humping them until they come their heads off. That's what I like and that's what I want to spend my free time looking at.' That's the kind of country I wish I lived in.

No response.

Not Jeb Bush's Florida.

No response.

Not fucking Israel.

No response.

I think I have worms.

No response.

Sometimes I think I prefer porn to actually having sex. Do you ever worry about that?

Harper   No.

No response.

Mickey   I've drunk too much coffee.

Harper   Have you?

Mickey   It makes me want to piss all the time. My bladder's shrinking. Does that happen to people? Because that's the last thing I need at this exact point in time.

No response.

Are you Jewish, Harper?

Harper   No.

Mickey   Is that a Jewish name?

Harper   Does it sound like a Jewish name?

Mickey   I hate the Jews. There, I've said it out loud now.

She looks at him.

Harper   Why do you hate Jews, Michael?

Mickey   Just 'cause. Fucking. Don't you? All that money. All those beards. Nodding their heads up against the Wailing Wall.

No response.

If I was there I'd grab their fucking skull caps and smash them right fucking into the thing. Stick that up your pre-emptive strike and smoke it, you fascist fuck-head.

No response.

You can't move for them round me. With their fucking, their funny fucking clothes. And the way they move their little heads. And their bangs and their beards and their stupid little weasel eyes because they spend too much time fucking inside listening to their fucking music and they never fucking clean. Get a bath, mate, you know what I mean?

No response.

I don't give a fuck about Belsen. I don't give a fuck about Auschwitz. Frankly. We've been living under that shadow for too fucking long now and I have to say this – there were worse atrocities. Worse things happened to other people. They just didn't own quite so many news corporations.

She looks at him.

Harper   I'm not Jewish.

He drains his drink.

Pause.

Mickey   No. I have to say. It is fucking good to meet you. I've always enjoyed meeting new people, me.

Some time.

She drinks.

Harper   I like your jacket.

Mickey   What?

Harper   I've always wanted a jacket like that. Can I try it on?

Mickey   Sure.

He takes his jacket off. He passes it to her.

She tries it on.

Harper   What do you think?

Mickey   It suits you.

Harper   Do you think so?

Mickey   It looks better on you than it does on me.

Harper   Ha!

She drinks.

Then turns to look at him

Mickey   You have spectacular eyes, Harper, has anybody ever told you that?

Harper   No.

Mickey   And they look fucking great in my jacket.

She smiles at him.

It's mad. Isn't it?

Harper   What?

Mickey   The things we do.

Harper   Yeah.

Mickey   The shortness of everything. We live. We die. We want stuff. And we throw a few punches on the way. None of them change anything. None of them make us feel any better, but we seem to do it and to keep on doing it. Christ. I'd bomb a few apartment blocks if I could.

She smiles. Drinks.

They do know I hate them, you know. My mum and dad. My dad told me about it. He choked up a bit.

She finishes her drink.

What do you think?

Should we go?

Harper   Go?

Mickey   You could come back to my place if you want. My brother's in, but he won't mind. Or we could get a hotel room if you'd prefer. They're fucking cheap round here. Cheaper than a cab half the time. I bet we could find one we could rent for the afternoon and all. Sometimes you can get away without paying.

Harper   You smell of whisky. Your aftershave is horrible. It's eleven o'clock in the morning, Michael. It's not that I'm averse to it, sweetheart, but you just stink.

He glares at her.

Mickey   Cunt.

Harper   Yeah.

Mickey   Whore.

Harper   Be quiet.

Mickey   Cock-tease.

Harper   Mickey.

Mickey   What?

She points.

Harper   Look over there.

Mickey   What?

He turns to look where she's pointing. When he does she pushes her wine glass into his neck.

He screams. He holds his neck.

She walks out. She doesn't give him his jacket back.

He stands up. He steadies himself. He staunches his blood with his hand.
He sits back down again.

Scene Seven

A beautiful hotel room in central Manchester.

Harper Regan *and* **James Fortune**.

She is wearing **Mickey**'s *leather jacket.*

She looks at **James** *for a while before she speaks.*

Harper   I just walked out. He put his hand to his neck. You could see the blood coming from between his fingers. His face went white. There was nobody around. He went to move and then sat down again.

A slight pause.

He'll be fine.

A slight pause.

I rang an ambulance. I don't think I hurt him properly.

A slight pause.

It felt fucking amazing.

A slight pause.

I probably shouldn't say that out loud, should I?

James   Are you sure you're all right?

Harper   I am. I am. I am. I am.

James   That's good.

A slight pause.

Harper   Has it been raining?

James   It poured down. I read, on the BBC, it rained sixteen millimetres of rainfall in about ten minutes.

Harper   I didn't see.

A slight pause.

Nobody knows I'm here.

James   I'm sorry?

Harper   At home. Nobody knows I'm in Manchester.

James   Right.

Harper   I'm married.

James   You said that.

Harper   I just walked out. Some masonry nearly fell on my head. It could have killed me. I kept walking. I went to the airport. I didn't tell anybody.

James   Right.

Harper   I don't live round here any more.

James   No.

Harper   I live just outside London.

James   That's right. In Uxbridge?

Harper   Some people think it's not really London. They think it doesn't count. Somebody said it's got all of the bad things about London and none of the good things. I go into London sometimes. I don't really like it. I tell people that I do, but I'm lying. Listen to me. I'm wittering on, aren't I?

James   Not really.

A longer pause.

Harper   You've got very beautiful skin.

James   Thank you.

Harper   Can I touch you?

James   Of course you can.

Tentatively she goes to him and touches his face with her hand.

Harper   It's lovely.

James   Thank you.

She takes her hand away again.

Harper   There.

She moves away from him again.

My dad just died. He was in a diabetic coma for two days. That's why I'm here. That's why I've come up.

James   I'm sorry.

Harper   No. It's all right.

James   Are you sure?

Harper   I am.

James   If you want to . . .

Harper   No. I'm fine.

She smiles to prove it.

I've not been to see my mum. They were separated. I always thought they hated each other. He was kind of like my hero. I just want to . . . You're very patient, aren't you?

James   I don't know.

Harper   Don't you want to just go upstairs?

James   There's no rush. I'm not in a rush.

Harper   No.

James   Are you?

Harper   No. I've never answered a personal advert before. You don't imagine they're actually real. I read about the website in one of the magazines from the paper.

He smiles at her, gently.

I've never been to a hotel room with two floors before either. I'm rather amazed.

James   Have all your family come home?

Harper   I. There isn't. I was an only child.

James   Right.

Harper   He was a teacher. He was the one who called me Harper.

James   It's a beautiful name.

Harper   Do you think so? I'm not sure. I've got a daughter.

She looks at him.

I called her Sarah. I liked it 'cause it was simple. Have you got any children?

James   Three.

Harper   What are they called?

James   I'd rather not –

Harper   Please.

James   Seb and Charlie and Mark. All boys.

Harper   That's nice. Are you lying?

He smiles at her.

She smiles back.

Harper   How old are they?

James   Harper.

Harper   I'm sorry.

James   No. Seb's seventeen. He's at sixth form. He's going to university next year. He wants to study history. Charlie's fourteen. Mark's eight.

Harper   That's quite a big gap. Between Seb and Mark. Do they get on?

James   They do. Yes.

Harper   That's good.

A slight pause.

I'm sorry.

James   No. That's all right.

Harper   It wasn't very difficult to contact you.

James   No.

Harper   After I left the pub I wandered for hours. There are internet cafés everywhere now. I wasn't sure I was going to click on 'send' for quite a while.

James   I'm glad you did.

Harper   Yes. I bet you are. Sorry. I didn't mean that.

James   That's OK.

Harper   Have you met lots of people like this?

James   A few. Some.

Harper   Have you used this hotel before?

James   No.

Harper   It's nice, isn't it?

James   It is, yes.

Harper   Do you like my jacket?

James   It's quite striking.

Harper   It was his. I stole it.

James   I see.

Harper   They'll be able to use it to identify me. It's funny.

James   What is?

Harper   I didn't expect you'd be wearing a tie. I'm a bit scared. Is that quite normal?

James   I think so.

Harper   Aren't you?

James   No.

Harper   Don't you get scared?

James   I'm not sure.

Harper   Aren't you scared of anything?

He thinks. He smiles.

James   I don't really like spiders very much.

Harper   Are there any spiders in the bathroom?

James   I hope not.

Harper   If I see one I'll get rid of it for you.

James   Thanks.

She looks at him for a while.

Harper   Are you still married?

James   Yes. I am.

Harper   What's she like, your wife?

James   I'd rather not talk about her.

She looks at him.

Harper   Do you think she knows you do *this*?

She gestures about her.

James   I don't know. Probably.

Harper   What would she do if she did?

James   I have no idea.

Harper   How would you feel?

He can't answer.

How would you feel if your sons found out?

He can't answer.

What are they like, your sons?

James   I . . .

Harper   Please.

James   Half of the time I don't really feel like I know them.

Harper   No.

James   Charlie, the middle one. Seb's kind of gone; he's gone into a bit of a shell a little bit. He never talks to any of us. He puts his music on. Mark's lovely. He makes me laugh.

Harper   Do I look like her? Your wife?

He doesn't answer. She smiles.

I thought I would.

A pause.

James   Does it bother you that I'm older than you are?

Harper   No. I like it.

James   I like you.

Harper   Do you?

James   Very much.

Harper   I like you too. I'm just a bit . . .

James   If it helps I could, there's a stereo, I could put some music on or something.

Harper   No.

James   Or the radio.

Harper   No. I like quiet.

James OK.

Harper There's always something on in my house. My
husband listens to Radio 4 all the time. I hate it. They just
keep talking.

A pause. She looks at him. She smiles.

Two years ago my husband was arrested on suspicion of taking
pornographic photographs of children. He used to go to the
park near our house during the day when I thought he was at
work and take photographs. There was a little paddling pool
there. He was reported to the police by somebody who I thought
was a friend of ours. They weren't pornographic. They were
outside. He'd go home and upload them onto his computer.

A pause.

When the police came round they took his computer away.
When they charged him they told him that if he pleaded guilty
then his trial wouldn't have to go to jury and he decided that
that would be fairer to me and to Sarah. Even though they
were, he was, he's innocent. He was put on the Sex Offenders
Register. Which strikes me as a bit unfair.

A pause.

We had to leave Stockport because everybody knew what had
happened. Everybody looks at you. It's unbearable. So he had
to leave his job and it's been difficult for him to get any more
work. Because mostly you have to declare it. I mean, he's an
architect for goodness sake. It's not like he's going to be around
children. There was a job in Uxbridge and I leapt at the chance
because it meant that we could get away and the pay, for the
work that's involved, I don't have the qualifications that I'd
ordinarily need. But I don't really like it very much.

A pause.

I've never told this story to anybody before. Not like this. People
found out. But I've never told it to a stranger. To somebody
I've met since it happened.

A pause.

I feel very ashamed.

James   You don't need to be.

Harper   No. I know. I know. I know. I know.

James   It's not your fault.

Harper   I know that.

A pause.

I had a big row with my mum. It was horrible, because she thought he was guilty. She came round to see me and she told me. And he wasn't. He isn't. I'd know. Wouldn't I? Don't you think?

James   I don't know.

Harper   I would though, wouldn't I?

He doesn't answer.

I've not spoken to her for two years. She rang my dad and she got him to go with her and she forced my dad to say he agreed with her.

She looks away from him.

You can't even take photographs any more. What kind of a world? What does that . . . ?

James   Are you all right?

Harper   Could you open a window?

James   Of course. Here.

He does.

They stand for a bit.

She looks out of the window.

Harper   I bet you didn't expect this to happen, did you? Big bloody confessional kind of horror-story thing. Do you still want to?

James   I think so.

Harper   Because I wouldn't be offended.

James   No. I think I need it. I think you do too. Sometimes we just need things a little. It's not anything to be ashamed of. I don't want to go upstairs.

Harper   Oh. Right.

James   I want to fuck you here.

She looks at him for a very long time.

Harper   Can you sing?

James   A bit. Sometimes. I used to.

Harper   Will you do me a favour?

James   Of course.

Harper   Will you sing a song for me?

James   A song?

Harper   We could have a little dance. You could sing to me.

She moves to him.

Here.

She holds his hands to dance with him.

He sings 'She's Not You' by Elvis Presley. He sings very quietly. His voice is completely beautiful.

They dance together.

You're a good dancer.

James   Thank you.

Harper   You're quite light on your feet, aren't you?

James   Nobody's ever said that to me before.

Harper   You smell . . .

James   What?

Harper   Lovely.

James   Do I?

Harper   Gorgeous.

James   I can't tell.

Harper   What?

James   I don't actually have a sense of smell.

Harper   Really?

James   Honestly.

Harper   Isn't that dangerous?

James   It could be.

Harper   You could leave the gas on.

James   I check it about three times a day.

They dance for a while.

Harper   I'm not really very in my body.

They dance some more. Then stop and stand still.

She leans on him.

Before I came here I met, near my house, I met a boy, he was, he was just a boy, really, I mean. He was called Tobias. He was not much older than my daughter. I thought he was completely beautiful. I could have looked at him all day. I went right up to him. Couldn't believe I'd dared. I've not felt like that for years. This is a bit like that. It's a bit different, too.

James   Yes.

She smiles up at him.

Turn the light off.

Harper What?

James Will you turn the light off? I like to have the light off.
You know?

She goes to the light and turns it off.

Scene Eight

Alison Woolley (*Harper's mother's*) *house.*

It's Wednesday. **Alison Woolley** *and* **Harper Regan**.

Alison It's good to see you.

Harper Is it?

Alison Of course it is. Don't be . . .

Harper It doesn't look too good. You don't look too happy.

Alison Don't I?

Harper No, Mum, you don't.

Alison I am. It'll just take a while. It's been a strange day.
A strange couple of days.

Harper Yeah.

Alison Sometimes it's difficult to lie about these things,
isn't it?

Harper To lie?

A brief pause.

Alison What on earth are you wearing?

Harper Do you like it?

Alison Are you having a bit of a mid-life crisis?

Harper I think it suits me.

Alison   It doesn't. It looks ridiculous.

A brief pause.

Where have you been?

Harper   What?

Alison   Where were you last night?

Harper   I stayed in a hotel in town. I didn't want to bother you.

Alison   I'm your mother.

Harper   I know.

Alison   Despite, whatever. Despite, everything.

Harper   I know that.

Alison   You don't need to spend money on a hotel.

Harper   It wasn't a problem.

Alison   Seth rang.

Harper   Did he?

Alison   He doesn't know you're here.

Harper   He rang *you*?

Alison   He's going out of his mind.

Harper   I can't believe he rang *you*.

Alison   I told him I'd make you call him if I saw you.

A long pause.

Have you eaten?

Harper   Yes.

Alison   Do you need some lunch?

Harper   No.

Alison   It's nearly two o'clock.

Harper   I didn't get to see him.

A brief pause.

Alison   No. They said.

Harper   Who did?

Alison   The hospital told me you were there and that you didn't make it in time. I thought you'd have rung me. I waited. I waited up all night. I had no idea where you were.

Harper   No.

Alison   I won't ask.

Harper   Don't.

Alison   But you're all right?

Harper   I'm fine. I'm a bit shaken up.

Alison   Of course you are. I am too. We all are. Let me get you a drink.

Harper   No, I'm all right.

Alison   A cup of tea even? Or a soft drink?

Harper   Really, Mum, I'm fine.

Alison   You look a bit white.

Harper   Yeah.

A brief pause.

Alison   It's been two years, love.

Harper   I know.

A brief pause.

Alison   You haven't changed.

Harper   What?

Alison   You don't even look like you've aged at all.

Harper   I have.

Alison   You look rather light, rather airy. You look exactly like you did when you were a child.

Harper   I'm not.

Alison   Of course you're not. I'm just saying you look it.

Harper   You're very funny, you know.

Alison   Why?

Harper   You're very direct. It's a bit unsettling.

Alison   I don't mean to be.

Harper   No. I can't believe he's . . .

Alison   No.

A long pause.

He was ill for a long time.

Harper   That doesn't matter.

Alison   It's a blessing in a lot of ways.

Harper   A what?

Alison   He was in such a state.

Harper   A *blessing*? Are you being serious?

Alison   He was in a mess, love. His circulation. He could lose and gain stones. He never stopped smoking no matter how many times they told him. They had to take his foot off in the end.

Harper   I never told him I loved him.

Alison   No.

A beat.

I think it'll be next Tuesday, the funeral.

Harper   Right.

Alison   Duncan's sorted things out. He spoke to them. He's been brilliant. I don't know what I would have done without him.

Harper   That's one thing.

Alison   I had to get out of work. They had me down.

Harper   What?

Alison   I still go in sometimes.

A brief pause.

I'll tell you what's odd. All of the customers are all my age now. It's a bit odd that. I'm the same age as old-age pensioners. I mean I know I *am* an old-age pensioner, but somehow that's not as unnerving as being the same age as them. I'm the same age as grannies in children's story books.

Harper *looks at her as though she's speaking a foreign language.*

Alison   The thing is, what I find frightening, inside I feel like I'm still thirty. I feel exactly the same as I did then. I never noticed it changing.

Harper   Mum, for goodness' sake.

Alison   What?

Harper   I'm just a bit. You always did this.

Alison   Did what?

Harper   I used to hate it.

Alison   Did what, Harper?

Harper *looks at her before she tells her.*

Harper   You were horrible to him.

Alison   That's not true.

No response.

How would you know? You were a child. You have no idea.

No response.

Are you sure there's nothing I can get you? I don't mind getting you something.

Harper   I don't need anything.

Alison   I'm trying my hardest here.

Harper   Yes.

A long pause.

Alison   How *is* Seth?

Harper   He's fine.

Alison   And how's Sarah?

Harper   She's good. She's great. She's lovely.

Alison   She's seventeen!

Harper   Yeah. She looks like you.

Alison   Does she?

Harper   She's the spitting image.

Alison   Is she still at college?

Harper   Yes.

Alison   That's good.

Harper   Yes, it is.

Alison   Is she enjoying herself?

Harper   I think so.

Alison   And she's doing well? Her grades and everything?

Harper   Yes, Mum.

Alison   Does *she* know you're here?

Harper   No.

A pause.

Alison Watch her.

Harper What?

Alison I'm sorry. I didn't mean. I mean you indulge her. You can indulge her sometimes. You know that though, I think.

Harper Mum.

Alison I'm only telling you what's actually the truth.

Harper *looks away.*

Alison Do you want me to put the telly on?

Harper No. I'm fine.

Alison Or the radio. I prefer the radio mostly.

Harper I'm fine, Mum, honestly.

Alison I could put a record on. I've still got my old records.

Harper No.

Alison We could call out for some food if that was what you were thinking. Get a Chinese. I like Chinese. There's a really good Chinese just up on the Square.

Harper I'm fine, Mum, honestly.

Alison Always get good chips at Chinese. I like them better than Indians. I trust them more. Do you know what I mean?

Harper I'm not sure.

Alison Of course you do. Look at you. You should ring Seth.

Harper *looks at her with complete contempt.*

Alison What? What are you looking at me like that for?

Harper *can't speak with rage.*

Alison You can't turn up out of the blue like this for the first time in two years and look at me like that.

Harper I'm feeling quite angry with you.

Alison   What?

Harper   I am.

Alison   I know. I can tell that.

Harper   I'm feeling quite angry with you for what you did to Seth.

Alison   For what I did to Seth?

Harper   And I'm feeling quite angry with you for what you did to Dad.

Alison   Harper –

Harper   You could at least look as if you're grieving.

A pause.

Alison   Harper. Look at me.

She doesn't.

Look me in the eye.

A brief pause. **Harper** *looks at her.*

Alison   I think about your dad all the time. There.

A pause.

Don't tell me I don't know how to grieve for him. You don't have the slightest idea what you're talking about. I was *fourteen* when I met him. I've grieved for him for years and years and years.

A long pause.

Harper   It's not changed, has it? Round here.

Alison   When Duncan's at work I get his old letters out. I pour myself a drink in the middle of the day and I sit and read them. I do, love. I get the photographs out. Look at the way you look in them. It astonishes me, how young you were. I look at photographs of myself when I was your age and I look for traces of similarities between the two of us and there aren't any.

A pause.

Of course it's changed round here. You just haven't noticed.

A slight pause.

I don't deserve this. You never even rang me.

Pause.

When *you* were at school you were so bright. I remember when you did your O levels. What have you achieved with them, really? Nothing really. Have you, love, not really. And he was very disappointed too, your dad.

Harper   Don't.

Alison   If you were half as good at maths as you were at remembering the words of your pop songs you would have done all right. That's what he used to tell me.

Harper   Mum.

Alison   And he always thought that Seth was guilty.

Harper   What?

Alison   I tried to persuade him that he didn't know. He wouldn't listen. He made me go with him to talk to you.

A long pause.

Harper *shakes a bit. She steadies herself.*

Harper   You're lying.

Alison   I'm not.

Harper   It was you.

Alison   No. It wasn't.

Harper   It was. Don't lie.

Alison Harper. I'm not lying. Why would I lie about it?
He told me you should have left him. He couldn't believe you
went away.

Harper *puts her fist to her mouth.*

A long pause, and then **Duncan** *and* **Mahesh** *enter.*

Duncan The fence's up.

Alison That's terrific.

Duncan It looks good.

Alison We'll go and have a look.

Duncan Takes it out of you a bit.

Alison Can I get you anything?

Duncan Just some water. Water would be fine.

Alison Would you like some water, Mahesh?

Mahesh No, thank you.

Alison *exits.*

Duncan Harper, this is Mahesh. He works with me. Don't
you?

Mahesh Yeah.

Duncan He's my apprentice, aren't you, lad?

Mahesh Yeah.

Duncan He's a lump of bloody mutton aren't you, son?

Mahesh Yeah. No.

Alison *returns with the water.* **Mahesh** *doesn't notice her.*

Mahesh Fuck off.

Duncan Oy!

Mahesh Sorry.

Alison   That's all right, Mahesh. Don't you listen to him. Here. I put some ice and lemon in it. Are you sure you don't want anything – a cup of tea or anything?

Mahesh   I'm all right thank you, Mrs Woolley.

Duncan   Listen to it. 'Mrs. Woolley'!

Alison   Harper's my daughter.

Mahesh   Oh. Right. Hiya.

Harper   Hello.

Duncan   I'm really sorry about your dad, Harper.

Harper   Thank you.

Duncan   I liked him, your dad. He was a very passionate person. It was very infectious. He was very well-liked.

He drains his water.

Are you going to stay up until Tuesday?

Harper   I don't think I should. I should go home.

Duncan   Well, you know you're very welcome to, don't you?

The amount of people who've come up to me, who your dad taught, who've told me what a good teacher he was. I used to hate my teachers. Did my head in. He must have been quite something. (*To* **Alison**.) Are you all right, love?

Alison   I am, sweetheart.

Duncan   Can I get you anything?

Alison   No.

Duncan   Are you sure?

Alison   I am. I'm fine.

Duncan   Right. Well.

He refills and re-drains his water.

Look at me. I'll be peeing all day now. Won't I?

Mahesh   Yeah.

Duncan   We should crack on.

Alison   Where are you going to?

Duncan   We're in Hyde. We're doing some decking.

Alison   Lovely.

Duncan   Yup. It's a beautiful part of the world is Hyde. Decking all over the place. Very lucrative.

Alison   It's turning out quite nice now. Be nice to work outside this afternoon.

Duncan   Not bad. My age. See these muscles, Harper? Not bad for a man of fifty, is it?

Alison   Duncan.

Duncan   I'm her toy boy, did she tell you? I always wanted to be a toy boy. Right. Muttonhead.

Mahesh   Oy.

Duncan   Let's get shot. Will you be here when I get back, Harper?

Harper   I don't know.

Duncan   If you're not. It's lovely to see you.

Harper   Yes.

Duncan   You're looking lovely. Isn't she?

Alison   I told her she is.

Duncan   I like your jacket. Very Marlon Brando. 'What are you rebelling against?' 'Whaddya got?' You look after yourself won't you?

Harper   I will.

Duncan   I'll see you Tuesday if not before. See y' in a bit, sweetheart. We'll be back about seven.

Alison   Right. Bye, Mahesh.

Mahesh   Bye, Mrs Woolley. Harper. Nice to meet you.

Duncan *exits.* **Mahesh** *waits.*

Mahesh   I'm incredibly sorry about your dad, by the way.

Harper   Thank you.

Mahesh   My dad died five years ago. It was completely horrible. I still wake up now and have a bit of a cry about it. Comes in waves they say, don't they? Waves get a bit further apart. I'm not sure about that. He was lovely, my dad. I don't know what yours was like but I bet you thought he was lovely too, didn't you? Sorry. I'm always doing this, me. I've got a metal plate in my head. That's actually the truth. It was a football thing. I got properly kicked. It was my own fault. He's wrong calling me muttonhead. He should call me robot head. Tin head. Something like that. I'll see you again. I'm off now.

He runs off.

Alison   He's a lovely boy, Mahesh. He works hard. Duncan's very good to him. He's done wonders with it, out there.

Harper *turns to her.*

Harper   I just wanted you to love me without condition.

Alison   I did.

Harper   You didn't.

Alison   I did, sweetheart.

Harper   I wanted to be loved unconditionally and you wanted to be loved better than anybody else in the world and I think both of us really let one another down. And I think that always happens. I see it in Sarah. She'll do exactly the same thing to me as I did to you. It's completely inevitable. It's awful. But I never thought you'd have the nerve to lie to me about something like that.

Alison   I wasn't lying. I was telling you the truth.

Harper   I need to ring the train station. I need to find out the times of the train to the airport.

Alison   You don't have to go yet.

Harper   I can't stay here. I feel sick.

Alison   Please.

Harper   Don't touch me.

Alison   I'm sorry. I'm sorry. I'm sorry. I'm just.

This world.

Harper   It's not the world, Mum. It's you.

Alison   You know something? It really isn't. You know it isn't.

A brief pause.

Will you excuse me for a second?

She leaves. **Harper** *doesn't know what to do.*

After a while **Alison** *comes back.*

Alison   I'm sorry about that. I just needed a little bit of . . .

A brief pause.

I watched the news last night. Did you see it?

Harper   No. What are you talking about?

Alison   There were men pouring out of the backs of lorries. That can't be right. Can it? To pour out of a lorry and gasp for air and lie flat on your back like you're dying. And the thing is, it's blacks who have put them there.

Harper   Mum don't.

Alison   What? It's only the truth.

Harper   It isn't.

Alison   You're so naive, Harper.

Harper   This is horrible.

Alison   You're not allowed to say these things nowadays. You can't even draw a line. You can't even say, 'This is wrong, what is happening here is wrong.'

You loved him more than me. That was belittling.

You had these little hands and these little fingers and skin which frankly you'd have been a fool *not* to want to take a bite out of it looked so good.

I hated other children. I hated their snootiness and their arrogance and their parents.

If you go and you never come back and you don't come back next week and I don't actually see you again I'll still be glad that I told you the truth about what your dad thought about Seth because that was an important thing to do.

Harper *looks at her. She can't speak. She's shaking.*

Alison   When I look back on my life, I'm surprised by it. I look back and I think – those moments I didn't think about. The moments when I was waiting for my life to start. The ordinary moments. The deadening moments of banality. Those moments spent in anticipation. That wasn't me waiting for my life. That was my life.

It's going to be beautiful this evening. The rain's all cleared up. Look. Look at the sky.

Scene Nine

Wednesday evening. **Harper Regan** *and* **Tobias Rich.**

Harper   'And how are you, Harper?'

Tobias   What?

Harper   You're supposed to say 'And how are you, Harper?'

He looks at her for a while.

Tobias   How are you, Harper?

Harper   I'm good. Thank you for asking. I'm all right. I'm fine. I'm great.

Tobias   You sure?

Harper   Yeah.

Tobias   'Cause you're kind of going on about it.

Harper   I thought you'd be here.

Tobias   Right.

Harper   I had something I wanted to tell you.

Tobias   Yeah?

Harper   I went back home.

A pause.

My dad died before I got there.

Tobias   That's shit.

Harper   Well.

Tobias   I wondered if that was going to happen.

A long pause.

Harper   That wasn't what I wanted to tell you, by the way.

She smiles. Walks away from him.

A pause.

How have you been?

Tobias   Yeah. Good. You know. The same.

Harper   How's college?

Tobias   The same.

Harper   Right. The engines still a bit –

Tobias   I only saw you two days ago.

Harper   Is it only two days?

Tobias   It was Monday.

Harper   It seems years ago.

Tobias   What did you want to tell me?

Harper   I'll tell you in a bit.

A pause. She pulls out a cigarette and lights it.

It's good for people, travel, you know?

Tobias   Is it?

Harper   It makes you think about things. It can be a bit unsettling.

Tobias   I've never travelled anywhere.

Harper   It's not difficult.

Tobias   How do you mean?

Harper   All the motorways around here, for goodness' sake!

She laughs at him.

You can walk to the airport! Go hitching! Nobody ever goes hitching nowadays!

He looks bewildered.

How's your dad?

Tobias   What?

Harper   Your dad? How's he getting on?

Tobias   He's all right. He's a bit grumpy.

Harper   How do you mean, 'grumpy'?

Tobias   You're being a bit weird.

Harper   How do you mean, 'grumpy', Tobias?

Tobias   You know. He mopes about.

Harper   Don't let him.

Tobias   What?

Harper   Tell him.

Tobias   What?

Harper   Tell him, 'Dad! Stop it! You're moping about! It's really annoying!'

Tobias   Why?

Harper   Because you should. I never knew anything about my dad. He was a much worse person than I ever realised. It's broken my heart a bit, I have to say.

He looks at her before he speaks.

Tobias   How was he a worse person?

Harper   Just. Ways. It's a beautiful night. It feels like winter's starting. You can see all the sky.

They look up at it.

You know what's poisonous?

Tobias   What?

Harper   Regret. That's what's poisonous. Regret and fear. And guilt. They're terrible. And we're only ever guilty because we have these ideas of things that we think are true and you know what, Tobias? They're just not, love. They're really not.

A brief pause.

You know when you think you know what's going on? That's dangerous. The only thing we ever know is that we know nothing ever.

Tobias   You are being properly odd, by the way.

Harper   I stabbed somebody in Manchester. I crushed a wine glass into the side of his neck.

Tobias   For real?

Harper   He didn't die. Don't get too excited.

Tobias   Fucksake.

Harper   Yeah.

Tobias   What was it like?

Harper   It was great. He deserved it.

She smiles at him. He smiles back.

I've not been home. My husband didn't know where I was. My daughter didn't either. I've just come straight here.

Pause.

What does he do, your dad?

Tobias   He works at the airport.

Harper   What does he do there?

Tobias   Baggage.

Harper   Which terminal?

Tobias   Two and three.

Harper   Everybody round here works there, don't they?

Tobias   Yeah.

Harper   Do you think you will too?

Tobias   I don't know.

Harper   Do you like it there?

Tobias   Yeah. Sometimes. I like the engines. The planes are good, you know?

Harper   Yeah.

Tobias   Thinking about where they're going.

Harper   Yes. I always liked that. You should stow away on one. I bet you could manage it. You could go anywhere. Don't you think?

Tobias   No.

Harper   You could.

Tobias   Your body freezes up. After five seconds.

Harper   No, it doesn't. That's an urban myth.

He looks at her, confused.

Tobias   Nobody knows your Sarah. I asked.

Harper   Right.

Tobias   Is she a bit of a boffin?

Harper   I don't know. What's a boffin?

Tobias   Somebody who just works and works and works and never does anything else.

Harper   I never thought of her like that. Maybe she is.

Tobias   That might be why nobody knows who she is.

Harper   I see.

A brief pause.

Do you know why I came here first, before I went home?

Tobias   No.

Harper   I wanted to put it off. I mean, I did want to see you. I wanted to tell you something. I wondered if you'd be here, and I'm glad you are. But mainly I didn't want to go home.

Tobias   Why?

Harper   I'm scared about seeing my husband.

She looks at him, then looks away.

Some time.

She turns to him.

I was lying about thinking you were somebody else.

Tobias   What?

Harper   That's what I wanted to tell you. My husband hasn't got any nephews. He hasn't got any brothers or sisters. I don't know anybody called James. I followed you home. I can see your bedroom from my back garden. I've been following you for weeks.

Tobias   Fuck!

Harper   I've decided I'm going to do my best to try to stop lying all the time. Too many people do that, I think.

Tobias   Right.

Harper   Are you a bit frightened of me now?

Tobias   No.

Harper   Are you sure?

Tobias   Yeah.

Harper   What? What are you smiling about?

Tobias   You.

Harper   What about me?

Tobias   You're fucking crazy.

Harper   I am so not.

Tobias   Did you properly stab somebody?

Harper   Yes. I did.

He admires her.

They smile at each other. Then look away from each other.

A long pause.

Tobias   You know I said I didn't miss my mum?

Harper   Yeah.

Tobias   I do.

Harper   I thought you did.

A pause.

They look at each other again. Neither moves.

Come here.

Neither moves.

Come here.

He moves to her.

She strokes his hair.

Does that hurt?

Tobias   No.

Harper   Doesn't it?

He has an erection.

Tobias   Of course it doesn't hurt.

She moves her hand away. She smells it.

She looks at him.

Harper   Thank you. You should probably go now.

Tobias   Yeah.

A pause.

You're quite sexy.

Harper   Thank you.

Tobias   Crazy people always are, a bit. Until you get up close to them.

She looks at him. Smiles at him.

Harper   Yeah.

Scene Ten

Harper's *house*. **Harper** *and* **Sarah Regan**.

Sarah   I would like to say I was sorry about Grandad, but I'm not so I'm not going to.

Harper   Right.

Sarah   I rang the hospital. They were the ones who told me you'd been there. So at least I knew you weren't properly dead.

Harper   That's good.

Sarah   We tried to think of some friends you might have stayed with but we couldn't think of *anybody*. Dad rang Grandma. She asked me to speak to her. I said, 'No.'

A brief pause.

He was going to ring the police. He didn't.

Harper   No.

Sarah   He thought they'd just laugh at him. A kind of 'well, what do you fucking expect' kind of thing.

Harper   Don't swear.

Sarah   Fucking try and fucking stop me.

Harper *looks at her. Smiles.*

Sarah   Mr Barnes rang to speak to you. He did a funny kind of little giggle when I told him that we had no idea where you were. We suspected you were in Manchester, we said. We weren't sure.

A brief pause.

He is, by some distance, the strangest man in the world.

Harper   I don't think that's true.

Sarah   He told me to tell you to ring him. He said he'd be very keen to speak to you. I asked him if he was going to sack you. He coughed for about three minutes. Which I think means he will. He told you he was going to.

A pause.

Where have you been?

Harper   I've been in Manchester.

Sarah   Yeah.

A long pause.

The day after you left, Dad fell off a ladder. He was changing a light bulb at the top of the stairs and he fell off it and fell downstairs. I ran down to check he was all right. He'd got up. He said he sprained his ankle. He could barely walk. He could barely speak. It was nothing at all to do with the fall. It was completely your fault. You're a selfish, thoughtless, cruel woman and I never thought I'd say that about you but it's true.

Harper   It isn't.

Sarah   It really, really is, you know.

Harper   Don't, Sarah.

Harper *moves to her.*

Sarah   Don't touch me. Go away. I don't want you to touch me.

Harper *stops.*

Sarah   Where did you get your jacket from?

Harper   I –

Sarah   What?

Harper   I stole it from a man I met in a pub.

Sarah *is incredulous.*

Sarah   Do you like it?

Sarah   No.

Harper   Don't you?

Sarah   It makes you look as though you're trying to look young. It's stupid. We had no idea where you were.

Harper   No.

Sarah   Dad was beside himself. I'd hear him at night. He kind of muttered, all night. Muttering away to himself. In the morning he'd be up and about really early. Smiling. He'd make my breakfast. Pack my bag. He gave me a fiver every day. I asked him if he was all right. He kept going on about how fine he was. 'I'm fine. I'm fine. I'm fine. I'm fine.' It was like a drill. Ddddddrrrrrrr. He thinks it's his fault that you left.

Harper   It's not.

Sarah   No, it isn't.

Harper   Where is he?

Sarah   I don't know. You know him. Pottering about somewhere. I don't know where he goes with his days.

Harper   No.

Sarah   He's like a wounded dog.

Harper   Sarah.

Sarah   What?

Harper   He's not completely . . .

Sarah   What?

Harper   He's not entirely without blame.

Sarah   What?

Harper *says nothing.*

Sarah   What do you mean?

Harper *says nothing.*

Sarah   What are you saying Mum?

Harper Nothing. I don't mean.

Sarah *looks at her and can't speak.*

Harper Have you had your tea?

Sarah You what?

Harper Have you?

Sarah What? Are you going to *make* something?

Harper I could do.

Sarah I don't believe this.

Harper Don't, Sarah.

Sarah Are you going to pop the kettle on too? Maybe we could watch a bit of telly together or something. *The Weakest Link*'s on in a bit!

Harper Look. This is how marriages work. Things like this happen. They knock your life out of you. You gather yourself. You make it better. You carry on. It's not just one person's fault.

Sarah No?

Harper No. It really isn't.

Sarah He didn't go anywhere.

Harper *looks away.*

A brief pause.

She looks back.

Harper If it's any consolation, I really missed him.

Sarah It isn't.

Harper I really missed you, too.

Sarah Yeah?

Harper I missed –

Sarah What?

Harper It doesn't matter.

Sarah Why didn't you tell him you were going?

Harper He would have tried to stop me.

Sarah Why didn't you tell him where you were?

Harper I didn't want him to follow me.

Sarah Why did you even go in the first place, Mum?

Harper I wanted to see my dad.

Sarah You knew you'd get sacked.

Harper I won't necessarily.

Sarah Oh, you think?

A pause.

You know Dad can't work. You know how much money he borrowed. I'm going to have to leave college now.

Harper You won't.

Sarah I will. How are we going to keep up our repayments? How are we going to pay for me to keep –

Harper I'll get another job.

Sarah Paying *that* well?

A pause.

You should just divorce him. It'd make it better for everybody.

Harper Don't.

Sarah What? It's what you want. It'd be less cruel to him. He doesn't really deserve what you do to him, does he?

Harper For somebody who is so intelligent, Sarah, you can't half be stupid sometimes.

Pause.

Sometimes when you're asleep I go into your bedroom and have a little look at you. I hated going to sleep and not being able to do that. It was really horrible.

Sarah   Oh, please.

Harper   Sarah.

Sarah   Give us a fucking break!

Harper   Don't.

Sarah   You sentimental, self-serving, sanctimonious –

Harper   What?

Sarah   When you were away, Dad said I was really like you. I could've thumped him in the face. I'd rather be compared to Condoleezza Rice.

Harper *laughs involuntarily a bit. Then stops when* **Sarah** *doesn't join in.*

Some time.

Harper   Do you remember when the police came round, Sarah?

Sarah   What has that got to do with anything?

Harper   Do you remember when they knocked on the door?

Sarah   Don't. Stop it. Now.

Harper   Do you know how old the girls in the photographs were? They were ten. Do you think he was really innocent?

Sarah   What?

Harper   In your heart do you really think he didn't take those photographs on purpose?

Sarah   I don't believe this.

Harper   Do you think he never looked at them when he was on his own?

Sarah   Don't.

Harper   Because I'm not sure any more. I think he might have liked those photographs more than he said. I think he might sometimes think about them. I don't think he'd do it again. I don't think he'd break the law. I don't think he'd look at the websites. I don't think he'd buy any videos. Or buy any photographs or magazines or any of that. I'm not saying that he's a, a, a. But I don't know what he was thinking in that moment and I don't know that he would never think those thoughts again. I can't go into his head. I can't prise it open and stop his brain from thinking those things if he ever happened to. Even for the tiniest moment. I wish I could.

Sarah   This is horrible.

Harper   It's not. It's just true. I don't hate him for it. Or blame him for it. Or think he's anything but . . . We act like idiots. We have the ability to be really cruel. Again and again and again. Sometimes we even realise. Sometimes we step outside ourselves and we look at ourselves for a bit and ask ourselves, 'Am I actually doing this?' and we tell ourselves, 'Yes, I actually am.' And carry on doing it.

A pause.

Don't you dare judge me for what I did to him.

A very long pause.

I know you want to know what you're meant to do with a life. Do you honestly think I can help you? I can't.

A long pause.

But, and you need to remember this, it's so much better than never to have lived at all.

Sarah   Do you reckon?

Harper   I do, yeah.

Sarah   The way you're talking.

A brief pause.

This place is splitting my head.

Harper *smiles at the teenageness of her daughter. She goes to say something and changes her mind.*

There is some time.

Harper   I like this time of day. I think this is my favourite time of the year. I like this city. I'm glad I came back.

Some time.

You should wear blue more often. It really suits you.

Sarah   Mum.

Harper   It does. You look lovely.

Sarah   Don't.

Harper   What?

Sarah   Say that.

Harper   Why not?

Sarah   'Cause it's not true.

Sarah *looks away from her.*

A long time.

Harper   How do you do that?

Sarah   What?

Harper   Have a conversation with your earphones in.

Sarah *doesn't answer.*

Harper   Are you actually listening to your music?

Sarah   Yeah.

Harper   Can you not? Can you turn it off?

She does.

Thank you.

A sound, off. Somebody is approaching.

Sarah   This is him.

Harper   Yeah.

A pause.

Seth *enters. He stands completely still when he sees* **Harper**.

There's a long silence.

Harper   Hi.

Seth   Hello.

A pause.

When did you get back?

Harper   Just now.

Seth   Right.

A pause.

I rang your mum.

Beat.

Which was a bit weird.

Harper   Yeah.

Seth   Are you OK?

Harper   Yes.

Seth   That's good.

Harper   Are you?

Seth   I don't know. I don't think so. I'm glad you're here. You look –

They look at each other for some time.

Scene Eleven

Harper's *garden. Bright, beautiful, morning sunshine.*

A white, ornate, garden table with three ornate white metal garden chairs around it. The table is laid with a full, large breakfast. The breakfast has lots of different colours. Orange juice. Some watermelon. Raspberry jam. White milk. Black coffee. Blue crockery.

Harper *is dressed for gardening. She is planting bulbs.*

Seth *enters. He is dressed in jeans and a polo shirt.*

Harper   You're up.

Seth   Yeah. Yes. Hello.

Harper   Hello. It's a beautiful morning.

He examines it.

Seth   It is, isn't it?

Harper   Did you sleep all right?

Seth   I did, thank you. Did you?

Harper   Yes. I did. It was lovely. It was nice to be home.

He smiles at her.

Seth   It was nice to have you home.

She looks at him.

When you were gone I slept on your side of the bed.

He moves away from her a bit.

What time did you get up?

Harper   About six o'clock. Maybe half-five. I couldn't get back to sleep.

Seth   Right.

Pause.

What have you been doing since half-five?

Harper   I had a shower. I made us some breakfast. I've been doing some gardening.

Seth   That's good.

Harper   I've been planting things.

Seth   What have you been planting?

Harper   I planted some bulbs. They're called Purple Sensation. Their flowers are beautiful. They're made of tiny purple stars. You need to plant them at this time of the autumn if you want them to grow in the spring.

Is Sarah still asleep?

Seth   She is. Yes. You know her. It's only eight o'clock.

He pours himself and **Harper** *some coffee. He takes it to her.*

Harper   Thank you.

Seth   You've only been gone two days.

Harper   Yes. It is a bit odd, isn't it?

A pause.

Seth   I remember when I first met him, your dad.

A pause.

They drink their coffee.

He was very proud of you, I think. I always liked that about him.

A pause.

She looks at him.

I'm doing my best.

Harper   I know.

Seth   It's not enough, is it? It won't be enough now. I'm being silly, that's my problem.

He goes back to the table.

Harper *goes to sit with him. She pours two glasses of orange juice.*

She gives him one. He drinks it.

Harper   I stayed at a hotel when I was in Manchester. It was called the St John. It's new. It only opened in the spring. There are rooms there with, it's like they've got two floors. The bed's on a kind of mezzanine. You have to walk up a spiral staircase to get to it. I was taken there by a man I met on Tuesday afternoon. He was called James. I'd never met him before. I contacted him through a website that I found in an internet café on Wellington Road. He was older than me. He does that kind of thing all the time. We had sex with each other. On the floor of the hotel room. I was surprised, because the way he made love to me was quite tender and I didn't expect that. I didn't expect him to be gentle. And afterwards I didn't expect him to hold me but he did. He didn't stay the night. He had to go back to his wife. I went to meet him after I'd been to see my dad. I thought it would help. It didn't. I think that was why I decided to go and see my mum.

She butters some toast and cuts some watermelon. She arranges three plates of breakfast.

He watches her.

After he left I was going to go out. I wanted to get something to eat but I couldn't face it. I had a shower and then I sat for hours on the stairs leading up to the mezzanine. The window was open. I could hear the sound of the street outside as people started going home from work. I sat there watching the room darken. I thought about you. I wanted very much to come home.

She looks up. The two of them look at one another for a while. Neither shakes the other's gaze.

Sarah *enters. She's wearing her pyjamas and looks incredibly sleepy. She starts eating breakfast without speaking.*

Seth *looks back to his breakfast.*

A long time.

Seth   One of the things we can do as a species is, we can investigate fossil history. I've always enjoyed that. We can also explore outer space. We can explore the stars. We can imagine other worlds. We can imagine the possibility of alternative universes. We can experience philosophy. We can hold a pistol to our heads in the hope that somebody will carefully put a hand there and take it away.

They continue to eat their breakfast.

I think I have lived too long in London. I think I'd like to retire to the countryside. I think I'd like to buy a house with a barn at the back of it with a loft in it. Take my wife up to the hay loft sometimes and sleep all afternoon. Our grown-up daughter will drive the car that I bought her to the supermarket to stock up on food for the weekend 'cause she's come down with her boyfriend as a surprise to tell us they're pregnant and we'll sit out in the garden and I'll have some wine that I brought back from South Africa and we'll drink it together. And they are learned about wine. My daughter and her boyfriend know things about wine that I never even dreamed were possible to know. Night falls. My wife is fifty but she still is the woman I most want to make love to. In the morning I wake up and my daughter has made bacon.

Sarah *stops eating and listens to him.*

Seth   I like the smell of my daughter's neck.

Harper   And the way her hair falls down her face.

Seth   And the way her hair falls down over her face when
I kiss her neck. Her boyfriend is a fine, honest man. He looks
after her and enjoys my jokes and never tells her about any of
the cigarettes I secretly smoke when I'm away at various major
European cities at conferences.

And the morning rises over Sussex and Surrey and Kent. It is
a beautiful day.

I would love her to see it. I'd love them all to see it.

They continue to eat their breakfast.

Sarah *rubs her eyes.*

She looks at them both.